Is modern democracy a fake coin?

Modern world is proud that it has democracy as its leading political system. This pride comes chiefly from the general impression that it is peoples own political system. Men feel a certain connect and belongingness with it. Unlike in the other regimes of the past, where third party actors like self-appointed kings, emperors and foreign invaders were in the rulers seat, it is now their own men on the seat!

All beautiful thoughts and beliefs ! When communist party came into power in many nations in the world, there was a similar elation and sense of proud among the class of workers across the globe. After all, it is the rule by their own class ! When Hitler came as a messiah in Germany after the 1st world war, speaking with great passion on the need of recreating the lost German pride, the entire people thronged around him to do or die for his great cause. We know what was the terrible outcome of such enflamed passion of the people of Germany!

What happened to communism also was similar in the world. Though Karl Marx was a true lover of humanity with great concern for delivering the poor and the down trodden from their miseries, communism had created tyrants not dissimilar from Hitler in atrocities to people and opponents ! The government that came in the name of the class of workers for their emancipation, had acted no different from the old masters that they had ousted and replaced, not only in deeds but also in matters of the bottom spirit of human freedom !

 The real liberation of common man had remained a larger dream under the new regimes of communist countries.

In summary, people were shown false dreams and ideological mirages by interested groups of power crazy men at many points of time in history, but so far no one has yet proved genuine in heart, for liberating the human kind without ay self-fish motive. There is nothing in front of us to believe that democracy was any exception from such periodical self-deceptions that history have witnessed !

The aim of this small book is to show the world how democracy joins with the above self-deceptions. People's hope stand heightened as usual now, but a general awareness of the hidden self-deception is yet to gain publicity.

The book consists of 11 articles written at different times. Each one touches some special area of the great ideal of democracy, showing what it was originally intended to for, and in what way it has been negatively transformed in the modern world.

As we have seen from the above example of communism, a lie and self deception can not stand for long. The natural dissent of people will cause its fall in the maturity of time. But in the case of democracy, mankind can not allow its permanent fall because, it is said to be the last of man's political systems. He need not expect any thing more advanced than a system of government of the people.

Hence, what we can do best with the democracy is to REINVENT it, to suit the genuine aspirations of mankind. We need to save it from its current self-deceptions, and transform it into a no nonsense, plain, straight system of governance of genuine people's wisdom and sense of reason. Hope this small book would mark a beginning. Let hundreds of such books and thoughts emerge from many other sources also, from people with wisdom and common sense , so that at least our next generation would see a really transformed democracy, fit for our enlightened age.

Author

Author information:

Abraham J. Palakudy,
Founder secretary of a philosophic non-profit organization; 'Conscience of the society'

(Conscience of the society stands for CAUSES such as freelance research and studies into the human faculty of reason, and that of a 'reinvented democracy' and reinvented media)
Web site : www.conscienceofthesociety.com
E.Mail : ajoseph1@rediffmail.com

List of articles with page numbers.

- This paper has been accepted by the 'International Society for Social Dialogue', (ISUD) a global body of thinkers and philosophers based at Athens, Greece, for presentation during their 9th annual Congress scheduled in June, 2012.

Democratic Culture: Historical Reflections and Modern Transformations*

An abstract of the theme:

The self-deception of our age with what we celebrate in the name of 'DEMOCRACY' is the biggest blot on its sense of reason. What the world persevere as 'DEMOCRACY' is nothing but an establishment in the old line of authoritarian regimes of Kings, Feudal Lords and Foreign invaders, except that those who are in the driver's seats are men from our own species of 'people'. There may be many external symbolic differences between the old regimes and today's democracy, but the internal motivational energies, and the spirit of the ruler and the ruled, are mostly the same. The one marked difference is that, in DEMOCRACY, people have more rights to cry out openly regarding injustices and inequalities. But such expressions of dissent also stand highly institutionalized that, it does not alter the internal working of the system in any degree, but only adds to its severity. Such dissents are also treated as essential ingredients of the false system and hence it offers adequate cover for oppressing of the regime.

Democracy was a 'quality' like LIBERTY and EQUALITY that evolved out of 'human reason', in the evolutionary maturity of time. These qualities were meant to redefine life in better and more civilized ways. But such intended meaning and goals of democracy have got totally distorted today. Democracy is more a meaning encompassing the fight among the members of public, or to be more specific, members of professional groups called 'political parties', to grab such seats of power in the governance of a country that the masters of the old regimes had once abandoned and has much less to do with providing the above essential qualities to re-define human lives.

The most disturbing tragedy about it is that, there is no general awareness of this historical self-deception among people, thanks to an excessively conforming media that exists in present time. Media has woven its magical institutional web around such a democracy that, the world does believe, what we have amongst us is the real stuff ! Moreover, by their projecting the peoples' expressions of dissent, a general feeling of SOCIAL JUSTICE is falsely spread in modern democratic societies.

The onus of responsibility thus lies on us, the ones who represent what ever is OPEN about humanity, to do whatever we can, to expose the self-deception about the last of man's political systems, in order to redefine human lives.

* This article was accepted and recognized by the International Society for Universal Dialogue,(ISUD)a prestigious body of thinkers and philosophers from across the globe. ISUD is based in Athens, Greece, and this article is scheduled to be presented at their 9th international Congress, scheduled to be held at Olympia, Greece, from June 22-27th,2012

Democratic Culture: Historical Reflections and Modern Transformations

The ancients had a distinct and clear idea about what they meant by Democracy. During the period of Pericles the Great, (490-423.BC) their attempt to define democracy was recorded as follows: (*Historian Thucydides: Pericles' funeral address*)

" Our form of government is called a democracy because a sense of freedom regulates our day-to-day life with each other. We do not flare up in anger at our neighbor if he does what he likes. And we do not show the kind of silent disapproval that causes pain in others, even though it is not a direct accusation. In our private affairs, then, we are tolerant and avoid giving offense. But in public affairs, we take great care not to break law because of the deep respect we have for them. We give obedience to the men who hold public office from year to year. And we pay special regard to those laws that are for the protection of the oppressed and to all the unwritten laws that we know bring disgrace upon the transgressor when they are broken. And we are also taught to observe those unwritten laws whose sanction lies only in the universal feeling of what is right...."

When one observes the above description of democracy of the ancients, what bewilders us is that, more than the administrative technicalities of the system, it talks more about how man lives under democracy. Including the general sense of Freedom, tolerance towards another, respect for the law, special protection of the oppressed, the universal sense of right and wrong etc. are more than what one could expect from a political system of people! The root substance and spirit of democracy is aptly clear from the above account.

Leaving aside the above version of democracy of ancient Greece, let us check our hearts for what democracy should be. The answer will also be on the same lines, because, as rightly observed by the ancient Greece, our 'Universal feeling of right' would also consent. The world need not refer to any other book of knowledge to find what genuine democracy should be.

Democratic ideals had evolved in the world after many centuries of suffering by the people, under the authoritarian regimes of brute, alien rulers. There was no concept of the will, or the consent of people. The most outstanding evil factor about such governments was the power and arbitrary authority evolved around such establishments. The kings and his counterparts enjoyed a status and authority similar to that of the almighty God on earth.

Hence, what was most desired by men when they had created democratic traditions was a system of collective living, where the collective wisdom of all men manage the job of keeping the law and order in a society, instead of the old evil of state authority. The state as a coercive institution was what democracy wanted to eradicate. Hence, they sat together to make laws, to control the conduct of all men, a document that reflected the collective wisdom and reason of people, replacing the old concept of arbitrary authority vested in the hands of the state.

This vital shift in the controlling FUEL of democracy is well evident from the accounts of ancient democracy of Greece. The substance and spirit of the great ideal was more central than its various administrative and technical aspects.

But some how or the other, modern democracy has got transformed more around the same old evil that people suffered through out the ages i.e. an arbitrary state mechanism, with the only difference that it is now run by a species of people! What we have today in the name of democracy is the same old type of establishment that the world had during the time of the Kings and his likes, with all coercive paraphernalia such as prisons, brutal police force, hand-cuffs, arbitrary arrest of citizens etc. Some prominent symbols of democracy such as periodical elections, political parties and a so called free media have come to occupy the centre stage, throwing the substance and spirit into the dust bin.

It appears that this fall of democracy into the wrong mould had not happened very late in history because barely half a century after Pericles, Plato in his 'Dialogue' (Protagoras) puts forth his frank admission about the democracy of his time.

"Its basic principle is the equal right of all to hold office and determine public policy. This is at first glance a delightful arrangement; it becomes disastrous because the people are not properly equipped by education to select the best rulers and wisest courses. As to the people they have no understanding, and only repeat what their rulers are pleased to tell them. Mob-rule is a rough sea for the ship of state to ride; every wind of oratory stirs up the waters and deflects the course"

We can not, by any means refute that, the democracy of our time is not any thing vastly different from what Plato had described some 2000 years ago! So, it is evident without any doubt that Democracy had fallen in the hands of the same old class of people, whose mind set was not different from those who had ruled the world at every age in ancient history, prior to its emergence in the world! Democracy has become a convenient ploy in the hands of professional members of our own species of people, to do what the kings, feudal lords, invaders, and tyrants had done for ages together in history.

The most unfortunate aspect is that the new class is doing it with an aura of legitimacy, because the evil system is run 'By the people, of the people and for the people'! Can a heinous act like rape gains legitimacy when it is committed by victim's own family members ?

Today, the definition of democracy has been narrowed down to certain visible symbols of the great ideal. The original substance and spirit that its ancient visionaries had set-forth, and what every thinking man's un-written 'sense of right and wrong' insists is totally absent from today's democracy. It is in the hands of the professional political classes across the globes who keep it as a legitimate means to enjoy the powers, freedom, and privileges of their ancestors in history.

It will be injustice if we ignore the true revival of the great ideal once again, in the form of American democracy in its initial 150 years (from the last quarter of the 18th century onwards). The entire world looked at America with awe and disbelief, as to the wonder of a peoples' government being enacted there. The most popular account of this revived experiment with democracy can be obtained from the brilliant account of the young French Jurist, Alexis D Tocqueville, in his famous book 'Democracy in America.' He was sent by the French government, to obtain a first hand account of the peoples' form of government enacted there.

He wrote that while government officials in the United States behaved as **'SYMBOL OF PEOPLES RIGHT'**, in other similar democratic countries, they act like the **'SYMBOL OF GOVERNMENTAL AUTHORITY'**, an adept report that explains the key difference of a true democracy from the fake models. He was, more or less, greatly appreciative of the American Model.

History knows well what happened to American Democracy after its one half century of glory. The present story is not at all different from Plato's description. One of the great champions of this period, Abraham Lincoln, had left a not-yet popular, but a narration of his ideal democracy:

> "As I would not be a SLAVE, so I would not be a MASTER. This explains my idea of DEMOCRACY".

Unfortunately, democracy of today is best described as a fierce race among the species of people to become MASTERS over their own men!

It is to be believed that the story of the modern formation of democracy in Great Britain (In the 17th and 18th centuries.) was also a story of deception. The feudal lords had badly wanted to restrain the arbitrary powers of the King. After the industrial revolution, a new moneyed class emerged from the class of commoners, the manufacturer-trader. The installation of the House of Commons, comprising representatives from this new class was thus said to be a grand ploy on the part of the feudal lords to restrict the power of the King, in the name of democracy!

Hence, the self deception of our age with what we carry on in the name of DEMOCRACY is complete, and it is a blot on its sense of reason. What democracy originally had intended was the dissolving of the myth of the authoritarian state, but it resulted only in the passing over of the evil from the hands of one master to another. Our enlightened modern age must seriously debate whether a true regime of people is possible without the evil of the coercive state mechanism.

Current evidences of this self deception

Evidences are innumerable. The recent Arab uprising, occupy Wall street like agitations in the USA, and the anti-corruption uprising in India etc. expose peoples plight under modern democratic system. As the US citizens allege, our democracy is the rule by 1% of elites, over 99% common citizens! People are mere instruments and 'material' for the present kind of democracy to run. People are false symbols on the flag of democracy. They are merely swearing stones for its leaders in the rhetoric they often indulge in, to 'stir up the waters and deflect the course', if we once again use Plato's usage.

Every citizen-leader in the recent agitation against corruption in India (2011) has received one or another kind of governmental intimidation, in the form of arrest warrants, tax arrear cases, or false court cases, initiated by high level political masters in the government. Corruption, as we all know, is the making of illegitimate wealth by the political class and government officials. It is the next worst evil aspect of modern democratic system, after the arbitrary usage of political power and authority. Democratic governments' hesitancy in passing a law that restricts corruption was evident from such arm twisting strategy of the state.

The story of the medical doctor in India, Dr. Binayak Sen, who had led a movement against the governmental apathy towards tribal population in the country, was in the global news a few months ago. He was declared a traitor by the government, and jailed under many false charges. Furthermore, incidents of fake encounters and killing of men who stand against the establishment are rampant.

The entire world know how our western democracies reacted to the Wiki-leak fame-whistle blower- Julian Asange recently.

Such incidents and examples are innumerable in democratic regimes all over the world, putting to shame such atrocities that took place under hard-core authoritarian regimes in history!

Not only within democratic states, but also at international scenes we see a clear lack of democratic culture and values. Nations act as if they are no different from the old intolerant regimes. The attack on a sovereign Muslim nation in the recent past by a leading power in the world, based just on a false pre-meditated report of the former nation's hidden nuclear arsenals is in every one's vivid memory. The head of the nation was killed, but no nuclear arsenals found. After a war that resulted in massive deaths of men on both sides, the devastated and un-stabilized country was recently abandoned, leaving them to fend for themselves.

No deserving hue and cry has been heard from any quarter about the international injustice. The media, as usual, devoured the event, with a handful of stories for their readers and viewers. The human kind is really without a non-partisan conscience centre in the modern age, to evoke a true sense of reason and justice in world affairs ! But every man's sense of reason would agree without any doubt that democracy has transformed beyond recognition. It has no resemblance with the model that the ancients had envisaged, and what the advanced sense of reason of the modern age would accept.

Key areas of modern unpleasant transformation of democracy

The power and authority of a Police officer, or a taxation, or municipal officer is still the same as it was during the ancient times of kings and his counterparts. The police openly slap citizens in the street in countries like India. Selective intimidation and black-mailing of the citizens by the police and taxation officials are also very common. The spirit of the one who holds power (the ruler) and the people (the ruled) stands the same as it was during the period of those old regimes.

Our rules and laws, that were made to restrain the strong and the powerful from trampling upon the weak and the meek are now more commonly used to trap them into submission, as we have seen in the above examples. What was meant to liberate has become the very tool to chain them. Hence, for the common man, the relation between the state and the citizens feels more like that between the predators and their prey in modern democracies.

The lure of state authority and power were suitable for those old regimes of Kings and his counterparts, wherein the ruler had no moral or legal responsibility over the ruled. However, a government set up by EQUAL MEN has no business in utilizing such dangerous weapons in governance.

Insisting that a state wielding unlimited power should NOT use it would be like insisting that predatory animals should NOT use force in the act of preying! Power is the most intoxicating force for violating the rights of others, and it is satiated only when it is put to use in the acts of suppressing rights and subjugating people.. Hence, redefining democracy suitable to the modern society is the dire need of our age.

Albert Camus-the Nobel prized author had commented :

'An age can be called truly civilized only when they start sending their criminals to mental asylums than jails', hinting on the need of changing the predatory and punitive style our establishments to that of a caring, parental model.

This vital lapse is what ails the democratic system most today. The mad scramble for grabbing the governmental seats that we witness in our time among the species of people is mostly due to the dangerous attractions that people keep in their minds for such seats of authority once held by Kings and his counterparts. Every child in the world has grown up listening to such stories of the power and glory of Kings and queens, and it is natural for every one to develop such neurotic ambitions when existing political system offers close chances to fulfill these dreams!

Another central reason for men neurotically craving for authority in modern democracies is the failure of it to instill a proper sense of security for their freedom in the minds of the people. They, including the leading class feel that, grabbing a share in the state authority is the only way to safe-guard their freedom from assault by authorities, as well as fellow human beings. We should remember that the precise goal of democracy was to instill such a sense of security in the minds of every one in the world.

Politics: 'For whom the bell tolls'?

Modern day professional politics has become the art and science of capturing governmental power by the people, through the few established symbols of democracy, i.e. the periodic elections, wooing public for votes, and using all kinds of propaganda techniques to pin down opponents.

Instead of the old time players of the same game like Kings and feudal lords, the game is played now by our own species of 'PEOPLE', hence we reverently call it 'DEMOCRACY'! The game sometimes gets bloodier than what was actually experienced in the older regimes. How can the peoples' own governmental system degenerate itself into a mere war of capturing thrones?

The singular factor that carries the great ideal of democracy into the realm of absurdity is the political party system. The fight among political parties for power deprives democracy of all its intended good.
The singular goal and the sacred motive of the opposition party from day one, is to find fault with the ruling party and try somehow to bring it down. The chief motive behind every governmental decision would be political gain for the party than the overall benefit of the people and the country. Hence, no policy, or decision is taken considering what is rationally good for the people, but what gains the political party, and the leaders personally. It is the sad story of party politics gaining importance over country benefit.

The ritual of elections

Elections are the most exemplified symbol of democracy, which is enacted like a virtual war in modern democracies. People's choices are limited, like that between death by hanging, shooting or on the electric chair! They are helpless in choosing the best out of available alternatives. Hence they symbolically participate in the great game of modern day democracy. Political parties spend millions on propaganda, and intimidation to win elections. Fighting elections has become one of the most complex entrepreneurship tasks that politicians have to learn in the modern day 'state craft', enacted in the great name of democracy.

Influx of capitalistic values into democracy

It looks like democracy has learned its valuable lessons of such entrepreneurship from the currently reigning economic system –CAPITALISM. More than any other thing, the motive of self-interest is the key in the modern day democratic enterprise. Its economic gain of the entrepreneur is the key factor here too.

Democracy has degenerated into the rule of another masterly class in society that derives from the open nexus between the professional politicians and the capitalists. There is now a fifth factor for establishing any successful industry besides the classical Land, Labor, Capital and Raw-materials- -it is the political patronage of the industrialist. With out his vital factor in place, no industry can do successful business in our kind of democracy.

Ayn Rand, a very influential writer and thinker of modern times had rightfully found that, turning the concept of the 'politically free man' into an 'economically free man' in the later stage of the development of democracy in USA has resulted in the growing inequality in the country. Filling the stomach of citizen has attained more centrality than giving him freedom of mind !The same cause can be attributed to similar trends in every part of the world as well. The genuine Freedom of man has become an irrelevant factor. Feeding him as it is popularly done in refugee camps with the resources earned by the elite 1% is the new economic mantra in the new democracy.

Threat of dynastic rule

In many democratic countries, traditional politicians do everything to ensure that the mantle of power be inherited by their siblings! The power and grandeur they had enjoyed in the country is no different from that of their predecessors, the Kings and his counterparts, hence they do not want to lose everything after their time.

Statistics says that more than 35% of the present politicians in India are either siblings, or close relatives of the previous generation of leaders. Interestingly, an almost equal percentage of the elected parliamentarians are tainted with a criminal back ground, at least in India, the largest democracy in the World!

Evidently, being ruled by a special masterly class is gradually replacing the great tradition of democracy in the world.

Notion of equality has taken away the very dignified entity of man

In the process of providing **EQUALITY** for all, it was the dignified self identity that was wrongfully taken away from every one, under modern democracy. It was like reducing all the whole numbers to ZERO, for the sake of achieving

Equality !

One has no relevance in the country as a common citizen. Only larger groups, represented by its leaders enjoy relevance in the system, because numbers are what counts in a majority based system, and not the single individual.

Rousseau described this phenomenon of the individual turning into a group being, some 250 years ago in his famous work., 'ON THE ORIGIN OF INEQUALITY' p. 98)

> 'He pays his court to men in power whom he despise; he stops at nothing to have the honour of serving them; he is not ashamed to value himself on his own MEANNESS and their protection; and proud of his slavery, he speaks with disdain of those who have not the honour of sharing it'.

The individual citizen tends to become quite afraid of his own identity in modern democracies, especially in developing countries like India. It is like one's nudity every one is perpetually fearful of its potent public exposition! By all means this is the single most distressing turn apart from the other twists that has happened to modern democracy.

Democracy was intended to uphold the individual, his freedom and his unbridled growth, but it has actually resulted in his being treated as thrash! He has turned a commodity in democracy.

Media: The defender have turned destroyer

Media, the so called WATCH-DOG in democracy, has opted to take up this political fight-game as a means to entertain people, in a role similar to that of the 'bout managers' in professional wrestling. Such an attitude is what fits more in the primary motto of their trade to earn more, by entertaining people more. The larger the readership, the more would be the income from the advertisers.

Media men are not at all the agents of Reason in the world. Their mission is to report the 'reported' versions of all the parties in the story. Such specially prepared 'press statements' issued by political parties and other public men are not the truth, but synthetic statements for the consumption of the public, though media men call this peculiarity in the name of 'objectivity'.

Hence, what people get from the media is a synthetic world. The rational human agent, in the form of a liberated media man, is absent in the act. They have their own professional priorities and vows, like the vows of other profit oriented institutions in the world.

More over, most of the media houses in the world are owned by rich business houses, hence it is more being used to promote the interest and view points of the rich and the powerful. They romanticize these features as an integral aspect of democracy. Hence, people have no option but to join the entertainment, and enjoy the game. Media has narrowed the definition of democracy into its one or two popular features, such as the right of every one to express his opinion, right of the media to publish it, and the periodical elections. The element of rationality is absent from their professional act.

Symbols are at place; but the substance and spirit is missing totally.

Nobody exists in the world today to shout that the game is absurd, and 'the King is naked'. There is not a single agency in the modern world that could be a called its non-partisan 'conscience', as once mentioned earlier.

Hence, the freedom of the oppressor is complete in our democracy. Unlike in plain autocracy, the oppressor is invisible in democracy. Hence, the helplessness of the people is also complete. He does not know at whose feet he must fall for mercy, or whom to annihilate for securing his lost freedom.

If 'reasoning' is all about logically relating a universally accepted base premise to build on subsequent premises, conclusions and systems, today's democracy suffers from irrationality, as it has nothing to do with its long cherished, self evident fundamental principles that we have already seen.

We can not abandon the badly twisted ideal of democracy to its own fate because, it is said, democracy is the last of mankind's political systems. Hence, we have no other way but to toil for a reinvented democracy. We could reinvent the lives of men only by undertaking this task on an urgent footing.

The onus of warning the world about the calamity that has happened to democracy is squarely on the shoulders of the thinking minority of the World! It is in their hands to must decide on some way of action, in order NOT to leave the world ORPHANED, and NOT to provoke our future historians to portray our age as another stretch of the dark age !

Why reinventing democracy a dire need of our age ?

Various twists that have happened to modern day democracy

Democracy has got badly twisted and deformed in the Modern day that it does not resemble what it was originally envisaged by its originators. The system that was 'for the people, of the people and by the people' in principle has become altogether a different game. It has degenerated into a game for grabbing political power- 'for the power aspirant (professional politicians), of them and by them'. Its end, the emancipation of man politically and spiritually, has vanished from the scene in today's democracy.

It has become a means for the professional political aspirant to achieve his goals, i.e. to come to power. This is the most glaring deformation that has happened to democracy, where every knowledgeable citizen's attention should be seriously turned. From an original motto of being people centric, it has transformed into a motto of being leader centric. It has dissipated into an affair for freedom for a few. The General public has been made a mere instrument in achieving the formers' dubious purpose.

Another sad twist that has happened to the democratic process is the over emphasis on the strength in numbers. Instead of it being the reign of society's collective wisdom, the democratic process has deformed into one of people gathering together into different groups to bargain for political power. Though the purpose of democracy was to empower each and every individual developing into his creative best, it has ended up de-powering him as an individual, thus forcing him to seek out groups to remain empowered. An unattached single person is a null entity in democracy. He is quite vulnerable and helpless. The society and country have become like a human body infected with multiple cancerous growths all over the body, where every single healthy cell runs the risk of being infected.

This single feature of modern democracy is in itself a subject of a detailed, long study into its various aspects of ruin to the political body. Attaining a semblance of being considered civilized meant that man had freed himself from the animalistic mentality of wanting to flock together. Now, however, under the badly deformed democracy, the trend has been reversed.

Every one neurotically attempts to come under the umbrella of one or another group; be it as a beginning group of friends from the same locality who could assemble together at a short notice to thwart attacks from another group, or a group of local antisocial elements coming together to form their gangs for a collective operation. Furthermore it could also be the local wing of political party grouping together into a power centre of its own to influence the police and other governmental bodies.

If the above examples are that of a negative grouping of people in order to achieve collective strength, there are associations of residents, teachers, students, customers and even investors for gaining the strength of collective bargaining. Every group has its own epicenter, a leader figure, and his close coterie. This modern mob leader has replaced the war-lord of older times.

Even in a day to day street fight, one would see a grouping together of people around the stronger party and isolating the single, weaker and unattached one. It is very rare that someone from the group takes courage and stands up for the weak and the helpless. As a rule, everyone opts to stand around the strong and the leader like figure. It is always a real risk to be at the side of the weak and the helpless. Even the law enforcement agencies generally side with the elite , and victimize the downtrodden. It exposes one of the worst moral rots of the day.

After this tendency for grouping has been brought to our democracy, single, unattached individuals have become a subject matter of laughter and ridicule in the group-centric society. Group members who surrender their individuality forever, so as to enjoy the benefits it offers, turn into predators in hunting of the unattached ones, because of their hidden guilt and shame for their own lost dignity and self-esteem. They would indulge in all sorts of shameful deeds to please the leader, forfeiting their own dignity. The materialistic gains procured in the group compensates for his shame. These compensations can come in the form of protection from larger groups. Most important protection would come from the largest of all groups in the country, namely the ruling party, (the government).

Rousseau described this phenomenon some 250 years ago in his famous book 'ON THE ORIGIN OF INEQUALITY': 'he pays his court to men in power whom he despises; he stops at nothing to have the honor of serving them; he is not ashamed to value himself on his own MEANNESS and their protection; and proud of his slavery, he speaks with disdain of those who have not the honor of sharing it'. (pg 98)

An individual citizen is quite afraid of his own identity in modern democracies, especially in developing countries like India. It is like nakedness everyone is perpetually fearful of its potent public exposition! This is by all means the single most depressing turn and twist of events that have taken place to modern democracy. Nepotism is the price that modern democracy continues to pay for ignoring this twist and deformity.

This phenomenon is the direct outcome of our democratic government's fundamental principles' going very wrong. Instead of ideologically encouraging every citizen to stand on his feet, the governments itself encourages the formation of groups and show of strength to take note of people's rational demands and necessities. The second fundamental reason is the fear of every citizen to stand alone as his dignified self. He fears victimization at the hands of some or the other group, especially from the largest of the groups, 'the government'. Its agents often act as predators upon unattached citizens by way of blackmail and extortion. His life and property can be usurped by men in power using government machinery, or he can be bombarded with unreasonable/inflated bills for services like electricity/water, or a bill towards property tax or income tax/excise duty. Or if he becomes a perpetual whistleblower against such governmental misdeeds, its agents can easily bump him off in false encounters ! Every citizen knows that the above propositions are not at all fantasies of any sort, but naked, day to day realities in the modern democratic system.

Unfortunately such subtle aspects of rot in the society are completely ignored by our media and intelligentsia. Blind promotion of old authoritarian type leadership qualities even in schools is the order of the day. Real leadership was always considered one's ability to kindle the hidden greatness in the other person, especially among one's followers. But sadly, it is considered today as one's ability to form coterie around him, and encourage the annihilation of his opponents, while fiercely protecting his own position. Unfortunately, the latter example of leadership is what we witness in multitudes of our corporate houses, government offices, and even in petty business enterprises around us. Every one takes his primary clue of leadership from the mother of all trades, namely country's 'POLITICS'.

The above twist was the sad result of the wrong interpretation of the principle of majority that has crept into the democratic process. The constitution of the country was drafted by the collective wisdom of the people, by the best and professional minds of the country, but its implementation in governance has happened to be by the process of majority opinion. What is being touched here is one of the root dilemmas of modern democracy. When a blue print is available in the form of a well meant constitution, its implementation also should have been by using the same principle of reason and wisdom of the best of the minds, instead by the principle of majority opinion. In this process,(going by majority opinion in parliament) the essence of the constitutional wisdom often gets diluted and dissipated. Great deviations from the core substance and spirit of constitution often takes place in this process of going by the majority opinion.

Collective neurosis among men for gaining freedom

Another fundamental twist was the emergence of a collective neurosis among men for gaining freedom.

If we analyze the cause of violence of every kind to its fundamental ingredients, we can observe that it is either for revenging atrocities against one's or his group's dignified self identity (i.e. one's selfhood) or a powerful man's or a group's pre-emptive strike to protect it from the have-nots. Both the causes could turn fiercely violent due to the nature of the cause, being it (protecting one's honour) much more fundamental than the needs of the body.

This is because the chief ingredient for man's happiness is his not having any one above him to direct and dominate his acts and thoughts. While he will willingly adhere to natural authority in human communities like that of parents and his co-beings with intellectual or physical strength. The problem is with institutionalized positions of authority, such as the innumerable ones in modern democracies, much more than men used to have during the time of Kings and feudal lords. Especially with democracy's increasing dependence on industry for survival and welfare, the moneyed class also wields a lot of power and authority in society, pushing ordinary men to the walls. His natural self-hood is in constant threat of being violated and abused. Hence, it is man's basic happiness is what is under threat under modern day democracy. Hence, he longs for freedom every moment, and in the absence any easy outlet in its achievement, he resigns to his state of non-freedom. This state of general 'surrender' is the worst thing that can happen to an age from its political system !

Though all the civil society movements of man throughout his history have been spent trying to find a solution to this ultimate end, (Freedom) so far we have been unable to achieve it. Hence we have continued clashes between men, groups, nations and even civilizations today. Man's efforts are marred by his own fear of letting the other man be free, due to his primordial anxiety about losing his selfhood at the hands of other men, groups or races. To learn to accept freedom and dignity for the other person, and also the only means to end this neurosis for one and all, is the singular task of human civilization.

The ultimate medicine that man has found to ensure a dignified self entity for all men, namely 'DEMOCRACY', is also suffering from the same old disease. In the process of ensuring equality of dignity and opportunities, everyone who uses political power to achieve this end, first ensures its abundant availability for himself and his kin. He hoards it for himself and his group first, depriving all others the opportunity to share it equally. We forget that dignity and freedom is not a scarce item like food and land. Only what is scarce in supply should rationally lead to HOARDING! Hence it is nothing but a collective neurosis that makes man to hoard political power in democracy.

The spirit of the ruler and that of the ruled

When the chair and the crown of power landed in the hands of people from Kings and foreign rulers, the spirit of the RULING class also had to be eliminated from history. But unfortunately this evil spirit refused to leave, but possessed those who have taken over the seat of power. A new spirit of 'people' had not unfortunately arisen and emerged from the turmoil. Hence there was nothing to 'possess' the people's representatives to manage nations, except the old spirit of the rulers. A new spirit with the dictates of Reason and man's collective wisdom to manage his own affairs is yet to arrive in the scene. History is still waiting for this happy incident to happen.

Should old weapons like the fear of a ruler etc. necessary in Democracy?

Old notions of captivity, separateness, subjugation or rule were not at all necessary as the ruler and the ruled became one under democracy. It should have been like a slave becoming a free man from day one after emancipation. It should not have been like the slaves having been sold to another master. This is the principal problem of democracy that every serious researcher or reformer has to surmount first. The old fear about a free society as mean, brutish and jungle like needs a fresh review at least now, in this age of globalization. Our age must seriously debate if freedom is an enemy of order, whether man should be kept in chains for the sake of social order. We must debate seriously if democratic governments must continue using old weapons of fear clandestinely to ensure easy subjugation of the people's mind.

It was man's REASON and WISDOM that found victory when he discovered democracy. Hence, Instead of power and authority, the two old time myths under previous regimes of Kings and royals, it should have been these two(man's collective reason and wisdom) energies that remained to manage the collective affairs of man under democracy.

When democratic representatives of people wield power and authority, the citizen's freedom and justice would be dispensed to him only as a matter of MERCY ! No one can claim it as 'a right' when the government is armed with concepts of power. If not mercy, then the citizen has to PAY for his rights and justice. This phenomenon is quite rampant in India in the name of corruption. Freedom and justice is available only to those who are capable of paying for it. The government has turned into MERCHANDISERS of freedom and justice in the kind of democracy that prevails today.

Deeper aspects of human relations that true democracy need to consider:

The cosmic physics of man vs. man

It is a new door of thought that we open here. Have we ever thought how one's personality is made? In close introspection one will realize that he is what others think of him. When one's behavior and actions are accepted or rebuked in a certain way by the people in his circle, such actions and behavior become visible and in the long run, it gets cemented into one's personality. In other words, it is the other or others that gives you your entity. Your selfdom in the social sense is a product of your social interaction. You need the other, like a mirror, to give birth to yourself! One's ego may not agree with this proposition initially as it questions one's independent entity. But it is a firm cosmic fact that with out the other, one is a vacuum as far as his personality is concerned.

This fundamental principle of man to man cosmic relation should have come to play and redefine the fiber of social ties in Democracy. The way state treats its people, is the way the citizen feels about himself. Here state has the role of the 'collective other'. If the attitude of the state helps him to upkeep his feeling of self-worth, he, then would be able to treat his fellow citizens in the same spirit. If the state evokes fear and anguish in the minds of citizens about their dignified self-identity within state, it would naturally reflect in the general social atmosphere of the country. If the state wants its citizens to develop self worth, and self respect, its policies and programs must cater towards this central need.

Social Ecology and democracy

In ecology, if one attempts to extract the net philosophical content, it says that if he does not look after his environment it will cease to look after him. So, to be alive, one needs to look after one's environment. Just putting his neighbor as the first unit in his closest environment, the science of ecology would gain a new meaning and dimension. Earlier his first priority was to get rid-off his neighbor for ensuring his own existence and improved comfort. Now suddenly the law has to change. The environment will respond in the same coin as the way you treat it. So will your fellow being as well. The old axiom of loving one's neighbor can now be transferred from the moral platform to a scientific platform and applied confidently by modern democrats as their best suited social theory. This theory can be the foundational platform of their political system as well, in order to devise their policies and programs to conform to this basic principle.

Capitalists have also learned the lesson of looking after the other, though for the wrong reasons

A third observation that further helps to prove the point is the newly found wisdom of capitalist societies and countries in looking after and preserving even the enemy blocks as markets for their merchandise. This trend can also be attributed to an unknown conformity towards our newly found principle of looking after the other. If competition, mutual fear and hatred have not produced any good for the human society in all these centuries of history, why cannot mankind now settle for the newly found theory of caring for the other as the natural law of human societies? Why cannot we boldly declare it as the law for citizens envisaged by nature under democracies? Why cannot it be taught in educational institutions under government authorized syllabi?

The capitalistic extremist of our age AYN RAND alleged that what society asks from capitalists is ALTRUISM, a moral burden. While entrepreneurs are the only hardworking people, the rest demand a share of their hard work under 'altruism'. But the above theory of each one caring for the other under common sense and wisdom of nature can free the capitalists from his 'altruistic' moral burden. And from now on he can do it under a scientific principle of nature.

Why does democracy stand disfigured and not people friendly today?

Mutual fear has become the symbol of the day because the state which was expected to protect has, sadly, turned into the most feared object for the citizen. It is against the state that one has to arrange for protection first and foremost! This fundamental helplessness and feeling of being surrounded by predators are what makes one living in a democratic system neurotically self-protective and hence naturally aggressive. The ties between the state and its people have become more or less that of a predator and prey.

This is why most of the parents advise their wards against becoming peaceful and law abiding individuals. They advise them to be street-smart, aggressive if needed, and never to have blind confidence in the fellow-being who could be a lurking liar or plain cheater. Every citizen is paranoid under the present system of the democratic government.

As the justice ensured under the law reaches him extremely late, in some instances could even take up to 20 or more years, man tends to believe and adopt ways to settle matters instantly by the sure and certain way of physical power. Fighting in the safety of a group is always a better option, hence every group is ready to fight out the issues with the other group at short notice. It is an extremely simple logic that democracy was meant to offer protection first and foremost to every citizen, and because of its non-deliverance, people naturally turn to the next best alternative like in the days of living in the jungles; protect oneself by all available and instantaneous means, the means of muscle power, the natural leveler!

Is there a way out to liberate democracy from its ills?

If our democratic governments could liberate our citizens from the above primordial fear of not getting a chance at full self-expression unless one becomes a leader with some power, the maddening urge will subside in the long run. The medicines prescribed in the preamble of our constitution- Liberty, Equality, Justice and Fraternity- if dispensed fully to our people, not just in paper, but in letter and spirit in the act of the countries administration, in government offices of all kinds, both in villages and towns; in police stations as well as tax offices, the disease will definitely end in no time.

Concept of Democracy as a common wealth of everyone's unique abilities

No need to group together to have your say. No need to shut the mouth of the other to help your voice to be heard. No need to keep the other under subjugation to ensure your self-expression and freedom. You help the other with his self-expression and he will help you with yours! Democracy is a common wealth, of the sum total of everyone's unique ability and creativity. Democracy should not be understood merely as 'peoples government' instead, it should be the government of people's wisdom, reason and common sense. Nature has endowed everyone with a unique kind of individuality and keenly chosen attributes. The fabric would be incomplete with out all. This should be the conceptual principle of a true democracy.

Parental Model - the best and the most natural model for Democracy

A democratic government is expected to represent the sum total of the wisdom of its people, like the wisdom of parents at homes. Parents' wisdom represents the collective wisdom of all its members.

Hence, such government can play the true role of a wise parent over its people, overseeing the task of making the voice of every one in the family heard.

From the stand of point of this family model, the notion of difference or separation of the state from its people ends. During the reign of other forms of governments like that of a King or a foreign ruler, state was a distinct and separate coercive agent, alien to the interests of its people.

When an enlightened parent try to raise his family to its fullest potential, family being an extension of his own self, he will try to find full expression of his own personality as well as that of all the family members. It is the ultimate goal and meaning of his life.

Parental model of state could be an ideal lesson for any Democracy to understand what the state's true role, and what could be its fullest scope. Rise and growth of his children is nothing but his own blossoming of life. He does not allow competition among his children, but will encourage each one to help the other for growth as one unit, the family.

It can not be seen as 'patronizing' when the parents encourage the wards to be independent and free, and equip them to face the world themselves ! State, when it knowingly and purposely provide individual dignity to their citizens, it is not patronizing but equipping citizens to become fully developed, responsible individuals.

When the democratic state adopt the spirit of a family as described above, the leaders can proudly be known as ELDERS, thus replacing the current -some what repulsive term: 'politician' !

Be free, and make others free as well!

Freedom has not entered the minds of the ones who dispense authority in our democratic set-up, hence he is incapable of delivering it to the common man. Abraham Lincoln's personal definition of Democracy is worth quoting here to understand the medicine for this calamity;

"As I would not be a SLAVE, so I would not be a MASTER. This explains my idea of DEMOCRACY".

Very sadly, no one amongst us has abandoned the desire to be masters yet and that explains our inability to treat the other as EQUAL. Another foundational father of democracy, Jefferson, has said about the relevance of freedom which also deserves to be quoted here: 'Those who curtail freedom for the sake of order do not deserve and get either'. Freedom is put under curtailment by its enemies always by the argument in order. Order is liked by those who desire to be masters, but freedom is liked by those who do not want to be slaves, 'the common man'.

What should real equality mean?

Will Durant the famous historian said once "every form of government tends to perish by excess of its own basic principles". The basic intolerance one feels towards all others in democracy is caused by the excess of its basic principle of equality instead of giving everyone its dignified place and status in society it has taken away everyone's status and place in the name of equality. The first question of the police to you if you try to intervene in any act of his injustice would be 'who are you to intervene'? In democracy, everyone is expected to behave like an irrelevant piece of statistic, a faceless citizen. He has no name, no identity and no social standing, until and unless he is part of the political power set-up. 'I am no one then how can you be someone' is the attitude behind the natural intolerance in the society. Facelessness is the mark of the day. Wearing this attitude becomes a point of power after some time 'I am no one, so I don't care'.

The notion of equality should go beyond economics, and find its re-birth as complete equality of men in the eyes of every other men, not merely in the eyes of the state. It should mean a society with no masters and no servants, no bosses and no subordinates, no madams and no maids, no leader and no followers. Everyone would take pain and care to treat the other as his EQUAL. Every individual is unique. One should make oneself free from all pre-notions of superiority and inferiority with conscious intellectual effort, like during the post-slavery time whites in the USA had managed to learn it.

Our house wives have to strive to a similar degree to see the house maids and helping hands with an equal eye. The maid can be seen and treated like a professional baby-sitter in western countries. No stigma should be attached to jobs like that of a maid, or a domestic help. This dignity of labour has been some what achieved in European countries if stories are to be believed. No one, including Indians living in these countries back out from accepting such jobs as it does not take away his individual dignity. It is a total transformation of one's mind set that the notion of equality calls for. It is indeed gaining freedom for oneself; one's freedom from 'intellectual rubbish-ness'. It is not of liberating the other, but liberating oneself, from the remnants of one's mental primitiveness. When one is not able to liberate oneself from these irrelevancies, he has no logical right to cry about inequality at the hands of someone else. Only this kind of self liberation would bring about total equality that would in turn sustain healthy societies under Democratic principles.

The hidden thread of the 'civilized' progress:

Those who cannot accept the other as equal has to realize that he is less evolved in the process of civilization. The old animal nature is taking a long time to leave him.

Civilization is definitely a process upward a ladder in increased civility and not about the degree of destruction his weapons could inflict upon his fellow being. It was without any doubt, a journey from stages of narrowness and exclusivity to one of more inclusiveness. The freedom of man has been defined in more and more fine tunes with the passage of time, if exceptional events like the Holocaust and the world wars are ignored. Mankind was able to learn valuable lessons from each of these negative events, and move further, confidently. The danger of men wishing to be masters, or superior over fellow men on some pretext or other is being increasingly realized by mankind.

It is high time for the world to adopt Abraham Lincoln's not yet popular idea of democracy, replacing his more popular one in the mainstream (i.e. of the people, by the people, for the people…)

"As I would not be a SLAVE, so I would not be a MASTER. This explains my idea of DEMOCRACY".

A reinvented democracy must be on the above line of definition, to be compatible with the need our enlightened age!

Every one should be keenly aware of the above hidden thread of our progress in civilization so far, especially the institutions of media and politics, so that it work as a master premise to build-on their policies, programmes and deeds. Every act and policy must conform and comply with the above mentioned bottom premise, as a test of its logical correctness. Every policy and act must be checked and evaluated as to whether it conforms to the above seen direction of human civilization. At all cost, mankind must continue developing in the same direction. A reinvented democracy is the sole means for mankind to be on this track.

SELF CONTRADICTIONS IN THE SUBSTANCE AND SPIRIT OF MODERN DEMOCRACY

The myth of the authority and power of governments over its citizens is as old as males' supremacy over females. When man's sense of reason attained maturity, the latter myth has been dissolved, and men and women were declared equal before law. But the former myth remains intact even now, despite the emergence of Democratic ideals that declare democracy a political system of equal human beings. In democracy, people sit together, discuss, and form a constitution that is primarily meant for restricting the government itself, (of equal people) from using the traditional power of such governments over the member citizens who are equal participants in the governing process.

Coercive states were the sole threat for man's freedom, liberty and dignity of self in the days gone by. Hence having democracy without taking away these traditional authorities and power that states enjoyed for time immemorial was plainly self-contradictory. Insisting that a state wielding power should NOT use it is like insisting that a predatory animal not hunt for its prey! Power is an energy habituated for violating the rights of others, and it is satiated only when it is put to use in the act of suppression and oppression.

Hence, having a state with pious Democratic labels attached to it, and at the same time bestowing its disposal coercive state powers was an arrangement of plain self-contradiction. However, our modern day democratic states plainly suffer from this self-contradiction.

The chief reason for this pitiful self-deception seems to be the mistaken belief that Democracy should mean only running of the old state machinery by members of the 'species of people'. The strict NO-NO was only for anyone from the species of Kings, Royals, or foreign rulers - the old oppressive feudalistic class of society. It was wrongly concluded that when someone like them, (the people) from their own midst run the state machinery, such governments will not use the traditional governmental authority and power over its people. It will naturally be a government based on collective Reason and wisdom of the citizens.

No one thought of the inherent self-contradiction in it, as depicted above. How can an old convention suddenly change its colour without altering the very motivational energy involved in its governance? The crux of the problem was the FUEL that had governed the traditional states, i.e. its power and authority over its people. This fuel of coercion was the one singular item that was supposed to be replaced with universal human reason and wisdom, for a government controlled by citizens with equality. Men's collective wisdom failed to recognize that a sharp knife will cut and injure even if it does not intend to do so, because it is the inherent nature and purpose of a knife.

Hence, today's democracies work mostly on deceptive rhetoric to maintain its pious image, concealing its old interior anti-people and anti-liberal concepts. Mankind is yet to invent a governmental system that could work on non-coercive methods, fit for EQUAL CITIZENS. Only such a government would deserve to be called truly democratic. What we celebrate in the name of democracy today is only a self-deception in the name of the great ideal.

Article -4

How has Democracy become a tool in the hands of the RIGHT wing ideologists?

In pure philosophical terms, what we have as democracy today does not qualify as a true political system of the people, by them and for them, because in its basic spirit, it is a plain competition among professional groups and political parties for capturing the THRONE. Their goal is to enjoy its proverbial goodies once enjoyed by the masters of the traditional old regimes.

The old myth of the 'power and authority' centred government, that was fit only for the times of Kings and foreign invaders has not changed to suit a true government of EQUALS during the period of transition to Democracy. Hence the only reason why we should call the present system a democracy is that, the game is now played by our own species of people! The spirit of the ruler and the ruled, or the paraphernalia of the old governing system, which has not changed at all!

Democracy has also become a clandestine war between the only two distinct sects in the world from time immemorial, namely; the ones who think that it is the prerogative of the strongest and the smartest to keep the less strong and the less smart under control, and in the opposite camp, the ones who are destined to be the victims of this vicious mind set, i.e. the less strong and the less smart in society!

First model is the 'RIGHTIST' MINDSET of men, the leading ideology in the world.

This ideology is passively taught in our schools in the form of inducement to become leaders of men, and in management schools, as smart techniques to get subordinates under control in order to take maximum work output from them, and in the governance of a country, as smart strategies to keep the citizens duly subdued, fed with 'noble lies', and similar other items in the modern 'state craft'.

Politics has become the plain art of practicability, as to how to access the proverbial THRONE of the old RULERS, using any available methodology or ideology so that multitudes of men could be brought under legitimized control.

It is this old conflict that is in play in modern democracy too, as its reigns have been smartly abducted by the former camp, after finding the great ideal a very convenient means to play their game with some element of legitimacy.

Third time Turkish President Recep Erdogan has said it very correctly :' democracy is a train where you can get off when you reach your destination'.

The drama of election, the only symbol that is projected as the sole centre and crux of democracy by its abusers, is helping them to claim such legitimacy. When such legitimacy is achieved in the route of elections, and once the THRONE is secured under control, people's name is used as a mere symbol on their flags, to continue the deception.

What happened to our democracy is in line with many other popular institutions in the world today, including, unfortunately that of the media as well. They are not now what they were intended to be at the inception stage. Media was intended to be 'watch-dogs' under democracy, to protect human freedom. But they use the above described mockery of democracy as a tool to entertain people !

The society of humans is still within the grip of the 'RIGHTIST' ideology, a mind set that is a sure remnant of the old jungle legacy of mankind. Hence, changes have become impossible without revolutions of some sort to free the human spirit from the grip of this bloc.

No philosophy of life is visible in the immediate vision of the world to counter this mind-set of the majority of the population. Communists attempted one, (with their LEFTIST IDEOLOGY) but they also did not have anyone free of this old mind set in their camp, to set the political establishment free of the proverbial authority and power. The communist regimes that came to power in the world started acting similar, or even worse than that of the old regimes that they had replaced. The problem of non-freedom of common people had worsened under the communist regimes in the world !

A new philosophy(that is neither RIGHT, nor LEFT but 'STRAIGHT') that could urge people to discard their inborn, untamed desire to keep their fellowmen under control and oppression is the need of the day. Our children have to learn from schools that keeping the other men under control in the name of any social or political institution is not in good taste, or fit for healthy societies. A future true democracy can only be born in such future societies !

Article-5

Politics: For whom the Bells toll!

Today's world stands abducted by 'POLITICS'!

One's sense of Reason asks: **why should it be so?**

For the major part of man's known history, inhabitants of the earth were ruled by Kings, Feudal Lords, or autocratic foreign invaders. Then came democracy, peoples own political system, to manage his collective affairs of living by themselves. And with democracy, there arrived 'POLITICS' too in the midst of people.

What does POLITICS have to do in the peoples own political system of democracy? Without doubt, whatever POLITICS does is in the VACUUM created by the Kings and his likes, at the REALM of the RULING class.

While some of them enter the field with the genuine creative leadership, an urge which is native to every man, most others enter the field with the sole aim of satiating a vicious human urge; that of keeping large groups of people under their control and authority, like the Kings and his followers had done in the days gone by.

The question is, why should a governmental system of EQUALS, i.e. DEMOCRACY require a separate RULING class called 'the politicians'? It defies a plain sense of Reason.

A King and his followers had OBVIOUS reasons to engage in the game, even at the cost of BLOOD-SHED, to keep his throne, because those coveted thrones were the next best on earth after the abodes of God! Losing it to someone else was just unthinkable! So, blood-shed occurred naturally during their regimes. However, there is no relevance for blood-shed, and even more ghastly incidents than blood-shed in modern day democratic set up, in the name of having a territorial upper-hand? Reason demands acceptable answers for such questions. Let us probe.

Kings and their followers were virtually Gods on earth. Other than their own sweet will, there was nothing in the world to restrict their power and authority in their respective Kingdoms. Their freedom was absolute in all sense.

The first bed-time story that every child on earth hears is about some KING and Queen. Hence, the highest and the best that any human being could ever imagine to become in one's life is, to be a KING/QUEEN, or someone like a KING/QUEEN. Hence, it is quite natural that POLITICS has emerged in human communities as the art and science to fill this VACUUM, created after the vanishing of the Kings and his followers in the world.

But democracy was never intended to be a competition among peoples class for grabbing the vacant throne of Kings. If democracy was intended to be a plain peoples' form of government, where people elect their representatives to SERVE them in the country's governance, the sphere of POLITICS would not have emerged as a profession of fierce fights and conflicts among human groups for doing this painful, managerial job. At the inception stage of democracy, no one had thought of getting rid of the KINGS' kind of governing system from the scene, which was predominantly a seat of brutal power and authority. Such systems suited only the Kings and their followers, and not a governing system that comprised EQUAL men.

But unfortunately, democratic governments had inherited the same kind of governmental machinery from the Kings, with all the myths, and the spirit of the RULER, and the RULED.

Why should people pay the price of POLITICS for embracing democracy?

Politics is nothing but a plain fight among interested professional groups, to access the seats of AUTHORITY and POWER of RULING countries. Its mythological and proverbial attraction is excessively high, as described above. This attraction is ingrained in the blood of every human being. Hence, the bells of politics is not at all ringing for the people, and their wellbeing, or taking human beings towards more and more civilized heights. It is an activity for its own sake, for fulfilling a small minority group's primeval urge to become a RULER, or at least part of a ruling class. People are mere instruments in their relentless pursuits of the above NEUROTIC craving for converting people into a class of mute spectators. Politicians are slowly grooming in modern societies as another MASTERLY class of RULERS, replacing the old classes in history, that democracy always wanted to do away with. This was a calamity that democracy by default intended to get rid of.

These groups specialize in gaining more and more peoples support in the society, to grab political power, unlike in the past, where physical strength and warfare superiority decided the fitness to grab political power. Like a meek but dangerously desirable woman, 'people' remained the target of these groups. If it was capturing geographical territories in the past, today it is demographical territories. As physical coercion was looked down upon in the mainstream world with the emergence of civilian ideologies, MODERN DAY POLITICAL GROUPS are up for capturing the mind realms of the people, to establish demographical strength. To capture the mind realm, the strategy involves around the usual feeds of the mind realm, such as culture, language, beliefs, faiths etc.

Can political authority and power of governments over people be compared to man's traditional authority over a woman?

When the institution of marriage was established in human communities for the first time, it was simply to avoid blood-shed and competition over the target of men's chief passion; 'woman'. Though a man's traditional authority over women had never been formally taken away at the time of instituting the custom of marriage, this institution has gradually been matured into more civilized lines now, where women enjoy equal status in the institution of marriage. Traditional authority of man over the weaker sex has no legal or moral sanction or value in modern times. Reason prevailed over the strength of the wrong tradition.

A similar transformation over the traditional powers of governments over its people was to take place in the modern day political field, at the time of institutionalizing democracy as peoples own political system. For a system of the government of EQUALS, this traditional authority should have been put to re-checking and re-thinking for its inherent future dangers ! This fatal lapse of man's collective reason was the chief cause for POLITICS emerging in its dangerous 'avatar' in democracy today!

Sans its traditional political power, democracy would have more soberly evolved into a much more effective and meaningful political system, truly meant to manage mankind's collective affairs, in the best spirit of Reason, collective wisdom, and more centrally, his common sense !

Even now, there are ample ways out, but what is first required is the opening-up of our collective sense of Reason over the stark reality. Over its folly, the sense of reason of common citizens, intelligentsia, educators and members of judiciary must open up.

The tenets of political power of democratic governments over its people should be fully taken away, and instead, plain Reason must be installed there as the controlling fuel. This proposition might look plain blasphemy for men with naïve, RIGHTIST mind-set. But mankind must put its record straight on this at all costs, as this transformation of democracy is essential to keep the momentum of the hitherto run line of development of human civilization, which was a distinct progress from exclusivity, to more and more assimilation.

This conflict between the RIGHT wing men (who believe in the natural right of the strongest and the smartest to rule over the less strong and the less smart) and the ones who were victims of natures own urge for EQUALITY and all inclusive outlook, was a regular feature of man's progress into civilization.

The Americans fought an internal war(The American Civil war) between these two ideological groups, on the question of giving freedom to the African slaves. One should remember that, this civil war took place during the reign of democracy - - proving that, democracy in itself, was no guarantee for the permanent reign of the principles of universal freedom and liberty of man. The primeval elements are still predominant in human affairs. They are the ones now keeping democracy abducted in the world, twisting and deforming it for achieving their neurotic end goals.

Hence, there should be nothing unusual about taking up the issue of transformation of the political power oriented modern democracies into a REASON oriented, pure managerial form of democracy. Democracy with a professional POLITICAL class to manage its governance, hence, is an antithesis to the bottom tenets of the great ideal.

Modern day politics is plain competition for grabbing political power!

Politics is virtually the new avatar of the old King's time of frequent fights over the ownership of the throne. In spirit and essence, modern day political fights for government formation are nothing different from those olden days of conflict for capturing the throne. Who can overlook the frequent political killings of the opponents, and those who question the highhandedness of the government in India? Who can over look gigantic electoral propaganda, invoking caste and religious sentiments of people, resulting in communal hatred and riots? Who can overlook the frequent bloody fights between political party workers in every state, especially at election times ?

Who can pretend to ignore the blatant violations of personal and moral propriety of political leaders who make themselves available as commodities for sale and purchase during the period of government formation? Who can ignore the partnership pacts that being entered between political leaders and corporate houses and individual businessmen, for sharing the wealth of the country after coming to power? For modern day large business houses, relevance of a new 5th factor of production (besides the classical LAND, LABOUR, CAPITAL AND RAW MATERIALS) is undisputed i.e., such partnerships with the ones in political power. No business house of large proportions can ever think of doing a successful business in modern democracies, without first having such pre-arrangements with any political party.

The extravagant war between the ruling party and the opposition

The one and only priority of the opposition party in the present day democratic system from day one is to find strategies and sinful alliances to befall the ruling government. Even the most rational decision of the ruling government for people's welfare would be pictured negatively by the opposition, as if it is their POLITICAL 'DHARMA'! (pre-ordained moral duty) Newspaper and TV debates are used exclusively for accusations and counter accusations by political leaders and parties in the game.

The media's passive partnership in political games

The media eagerly depicts all these chaos and absurdities for the consumption of the citizens, as vibrant, inevitable features of the great ideal, urging them to love it, and remain proud patrons of the system. They have succeeded in romanticising everything that happens in the name of DEMOCRACY, and make people feel that everything is perfectly well as per democratic norms. For them, it seems, democracy should only mean everyone's freedom to air their voice, without any clear ideological direction. The underlying, hidden thread of plain Reason that had given birth to democracy, which should be the sole guiding line and spirit of its everyday course, eludes them for unknown reasons.

Their job in democracy appears more similar to that of BOUT-MANAGERS in professional wrestling competitions, than a no non-sense WATCH-DOG role in Democracy! They predominantly show the conflict aspect of politics among political parties and its leaders, as it has more appeal for their viewers and readers. They entertain people, showing the inherent conflicting aspects in modern day democracy. Their business angle of the profession keeps them away from the burden of leading people, and mankind in general, to intellectual sanity and clarity. This vital omission on the part of the Media is indirectly helping the deformed form of democracy thrive unchecked in the world. They could have saved the world, by leading both the leading class as well as the common people out of the calamity, provided they had the right insight, and the will to undertake the said task that was professionally expected of them.

Hence, the final question again; should POLITICS take an important position so that we could have democracy ? The game of politics and its motivational spirits and working energies have nothing to do with the role of pure democratic principles. Its bells are certainly not ringing for people's welfare, or the notion of a pure uncorrupted form of democracy.

Politics is the antithesis of the individual centred modern political theory

The most outstanding contribution of the Western or European thought to humanity is putting the human person as the end objective of all political and sociological theories. Every system of man must be aimed at serving the purpose of this human individual, his sense of self-dignity, liberty and freedom. The end objective of every state is the achievement of this singular goal.

Concepts like 'the inalienable rights of man' that took centre stage after the French and American revolutions have changed the very course of human development. This golden theory and the western world's relentless efforts on this line have seen the entire world now enjoying the fruits of their scientific achievements,(due to setting the mind free) and an overall human progress that modern centuries have witnessed.

Hence, serious doubts arise as to whether present day capitalistic-democratic governmental systems would be able to keep this centrality of individual dignity intact for long. Many of its latest developments and ideologies straight away clash with the 'centrality' of the above notion of human person.

The above described 'POLITICS' dominated democracy has no slot for the DIGNIFIED HUMAN PERSON in its scheme of things. They aim at wholesale handling of communities and groups, based on caste, language and religion. A single individual is like a low denomination coin for modern day political parties. One's status and value in the society is ascertained by the group he belongs to. A stand alone individual is a NULL and VOID entity in modern societies.

The independent mind of man stands dead today. No one is interested in developing 'free spirit' of human mind, a sole cradle of creative pursuits. We must remember, Renaissance, the collective revival of human mind had happened during the brief interval of its freedom after the fall of church's authority in human affairs ! That freedom was short-lived. After the industrial revolution, and the thriving of capitalistic-democracy in Europe and USA, freedom of mind found its new enemy! For the new world, facts, truth and knowledge is what comes out from the mouths of its new masters- -the capitalists, and their partner-collaborators; the political class.

The myth and fantasy of an OPEN WORLD!

Hence, an open world, as a notion, can be said to be a clear FANTASY, a FALSE notion in the modern world. The modern world is like a personal back yard of powerful countries, or that of powerful industrial groups, who have a clear stake over almost 85% of the worlds' wealth.

As for human civilization, a thread that generations to come will depend upon defining and finding their meaning in their lives, depends upon such notions of an open world, with a distinct and clear RATIONAL and MORAL basis. But can anyone pin-point such a centre in the modern world as existing? Despite having an organization such as the United Nations Organization to work for world peace and stability, a country like USA as the most powerful democracy in the world, a media that 24x7 depicts the world to its people; a moral conscience of the world is clearly absent. What we are made to hear is the voice of its strongest of MASTERS, who is interested only in making their voice heard as the final word on truth and non-truth. The modern world is an ORPHANED entity in all its meaning!

Enlightened generations of the future would definitely stamp our generation as another extension of the DARK AGES, because the human mind as a living organ stands dead today. The modern day predators in human societies are preying on the mind, not flesh.

What the world badly require are new values and new directions. It has to save itself from self-deceptions like its twisted and deformed form of DEMOCRACY. Democracy without the infectious disease of POLITICS is what the world badly needs, a straight, no-nonsense, people's own form of, pure management oriented governmental system.

Man's native urge to put all other men around him, under his control is an old jungle trait. Liberate the other person for sustainable freedom for all, is the key value for future societies.

Influx of capitalistic values into democracy

In most of the countries in the world, irrespective of the political system, capitalism is the reigning economic system. Freedom of enterprise is its hallmark. Competition to sell more or create a high demand for one's own product over that of the others is also its inevitable feature.

One of capitalism's great champions of our century Ms. Ayn Rand says 'Capitalism is the very symbol of man's ultimate freedom'. It gives the entrepreneur the ultimate expression of his creativity. It gives the same freedom to his customer, as well as employee too. They are also free to choose his product or his employer; an atmosphere of complete freedom!

But when the reigning political system of modern day-Democracy- has also adopted the above principles of capitalism for upholding freedom, it makes an interesting study. This turn-out has directly eroded the underlying sacred goals of democracy, and transformed it into a matter of entrepreneurship for use by political parties collectively, and its leaders individually, for the capture of governmental power, and enjoyment of its fruits.

Whatever is listed in the election manifesto are their products to sell. It is the product catalogue. It consists of the various goodies they would offer to people if voted to power. It also boasts about the calibre of their leaders. It offers not only various infrastructural items like roads, electricity, water etc, but also notional products like freedom, equality and justice.

These entrepreneurs attempt to influence the buyers of these products, using all kinds of propaganda techniques, including services of the top niche marketing gurus. What they want from people in return is their mandate, their life deciding vote.

In this fierce competition, winning is not only the game, but pinning down the competitor too forms an integral part of the game. It often moves beyond mere counter propaganda. It turns nasty, and at times bloodier than the battles for the throne that Kings had fought in the days gone by. Political killings are not something new in democracy.

Though under capitalism man stands reduced to his

primordial jungle like elements, the compulsions of the norms of a civil society has made him pretend his compliance. But this hypocrisy will bare its teeth the moment one reaches the limit of his pretence! There after, the world can turn into a jungle within seconds.

Capitalism takes all the care to keep the mainstream world looking like the well decorated lobby of a star hotel. The PR factor is central for every big business.

The most glaring negative value that capitalism has brought into the democratic society is the self asserted special rights for the rich and powerful. The pity lies in the fact that such assertions are always passively allowed by the less privileged, as if it is a natural law, though democracy was born in human society to replace this old belief.

Capitalism pre-fixes each one's place and position in the society as it was during the old caste ridden times. The citizen has a place, a pre-defined value, and a state provided identity. Anyone who dares to ascertain one's individuality over and above such pre-fixed roles will court trouble. He will run the risk of being branded a trouble maker, an odd man out. Hence, one has to bury his individuality within, to make a typically good, law-abiding citizen of the country, willing to carry the flags of his masters and leaders, whenever called upon to do so.

Like the unchallenged rights of the strongest in the days gone by, people have no option but to submit to the various institutionalized authoritative points created in the capitalist system.

There is no respect or relevance for an activity or a cause that has no profitable outcome. Only if some monetary return comes forth from such an activity or cause, it is considered worthwhile. People who indulge in such worthless activities are considered foolish and useless.

A natural outcome of this obsession for cash value is that the rich and powerful are always treated in high esteem. The world is at their beck and call. Such highly placed institutions in democracy including the Media are victims of this norm. They are too willing to come out with flashy stories of people who have made it to the top, as if to beckon the world to emulate them as shining examples of human achievement.

Universal goals like a civilized human advancement, by spreading the themes of equal respect for one and all in the society etc. are thrown up in the air by this sector, as this sector is mostly owned and run by capitalistic entrepreneurs. The media is helpless but to act as a passive conduit for the values and norms of their master class.

Hence the media always fail to stand beside the most creative members in the society, who usually are fiercely independent, never conform, or yield to the preferences of the mass. The Media never makes icons from this class, possibly fearing loss of their monopoly of opinion on social issues.

Like the political class, the media too swears by the voice of the masses, (peoples' voice!) to carry their view point home. They often represent, and side with the kind of mediocre crowd, who had asked their then rulers of Athens (Greece) for Socrates' death, and to the then Roman officials for crucifixion of Christ! This outcome of the media is the saddest aspect of the phenomenon taken up in this article.

Though the right to question anyone and everything is allowed in democracy, no one would dare to defy such a highly institutionalized authority, for fear of losing one's livelihood. There is abundant freedom for all, but the courage to exercise such freedom is taken away by these indirect methods. Thus, the free spirit of a majority of the population stands abducted, and consciously kept under check in capitalism.

Democracy has thus become a meek and obliging hand-maiden in the capitalist society. The saddest thing is that no one seems to be aware of this transformation of the great political system of people into a pure commercial enterprise in the hands of a few. Media, the watch dog in democracy has become the enthusiastic drummer and bugle blower of the system in its existing form, due to reasons stated above.

Democracy has become what its leaders do. It's endless, reaching no where debates, their fist-fights in parliament, their self-deception and double talk, all are well aired on TV, as well as published in print Media, resulting in the legitimization of all these acts as routine part and parcel of the democratic process! People are asked to accept it and feel proud of such legacies, because it is after all 'by the people, of the people and for the people', line by line and dot by dot, according to the definition in the book. Is it not time for us to revisit democracy's foundational principles ?

The 5th factor of modern industrial production

Classical industrial studies in text books have 4 factors essential for industrial production, for students to study; which are namely land; labour; capital; and raw material.

But in the modern context, a new, inevitable factor of industrial enterprise is self evident i.e. the governmental support or the policy factor of the government in power. This 5th factor is the central factor that every successful, giant industrial house cares to lay its hands on first before venturing into any large investment. Without having a firm grip in the political power sector, a link is often equal to a partnership; no sensible industrial house can confidently invest money in the industry. If anyone takes the risk without this pre-arrangement, it would be to his risk of peril.

Such partnerships are often in the form of huge contributions towards party funds of political parties. Or, an offer of directorship to some close relations of the minister concerned. This new face of capitalism and business partnership is the hall mark of modern DEMOCRACY. It is clearly a partnership affair between industrial houses and professional political parties and their leaders.

At a lower level, it thrives on such understandings and sharing of profits between the political power holder and the entrepreneur. (It thrives at the MLA level, a police chief level or at the level of a secretary in a political party. And furthermore at still lower levels, it can take place as an understanding with a factory owner and a Jr. Engineer from the Department of Electricity, for power theft like favours). It is an irrefutable reality of modern day politics involving democracy. But the mainstream world, chiefly led by the industry owned media houses, pretends to be unaware of it, and present to the people the beautiful images of an OPEN, FREE world, and a transparent democracy !

People are merely a means to cater to the institutionalized, electoral form of government formation in democracies. Elections are plain commodities, which need to be strategically managed using sophisticated propaganda techniques such as the electoral market specialists who first decide the effective 'electoral issues' for people and communities to consume, and then turn their mandate toward a self desired direction. It is a virtual war, wherein results are the only deciding factor. Hence any anti-mankind, antirational, and fantastic issues would be used to woo public attention, and the final product, the vote.

In the above scenario, concept of an OPEN WORLD is a mere fantasy and those who **maintain** such utopian dreams are foolish and naïve. But the media is in the game of making the world appear open and transparent as possible, in tune with such images that any average man has learned in his school text books.

The media was the only strata in modern human societies that could have safe-guarded public interest, in the world of the above witnessed silent secret pacts and understandings. But this sector has, as said earlier, mostly been bought over by the industrial houses, hence the traditional media interference and activism to save the world, also remains a fantasy and an impossible dream.

Would it be trickling down of the surplus among the poor, or sieving out the poor in capitalistic societies?

If the TRICKLING DOWN theory of capitalism was true, (the belief that the surplus wealth created by the capitalists would slowly but surely trickle down through the economic layers of society till it reaches the bottom poor one day, freeing every one from hunger and thirst) the rich to poor ratio of 75% of the world's wealth in the hands of 25% of the rich a quarter century ago, would not have been moved to 85%: 15% ratio as of now! So, it is a sieving out the poor and the un-desired is what actually takes place in capitalism. Those who cannot take part in the process of business are considered dead-wood in an industry, and hence declared useless. Those who cannot take blind orders from their superiors, and obey authority of the neo 'high castes', are also discarded as outcastes in modern capitalistic societies.

But nature is kind to all. She directs such discarded ones against their one time oppressors and enemies, in the form of purse snatchers, high-way robbers, burglars and even as sophisticated underworld characters! Terrorism is also an after effect of the same cause, but as a different face of the same sieving out from the main stream society. It has a rather larger geographical dimension, than caused directly by localized issues.

Sustainable peace will erode mankind till the world collectively learn the natural lesson of not institutionalizing relevance and importance of any single native ability of man over that of any other man. If those who were in the profession of serving God had an upper hand in society in the days gone by, followed by the institutionalized authority of the well-armed and well trained war-lords later on, now it is the turn of entrepreneurs in the world. Equality is yet to be defined on newer grounds.

Article -8

Why can't democratic governments run like pure managerial exercises ?

Why should our enlightened age carry on with a democracy as a political drama instead of having it as a plain managerial tool for running a people's government? Why is it not possible for us to get rid of its rhetoric and the propagandist deceptions? Why can't we bring an end to its primary image as a non-stop fight among political parties to gain an advantage over the other, while the rest the priorities of the nation fall back to secondary issues?

We have a well prepared policy document called the constitution to run the country. The philosophical, political, psychological and historical needs of a people are well documented in the constitution.

What we need is a representative team to run the country with the best managerial expertise, like the way a corporate house runs its business, or like constructing a building according to its blue-print plan.

Targets to be achieved by each ministry could be prepared with the help of organizations like FICCI or CII, or any of the top management schools in the country. Inexperienced ministers could be trained in the art of delegating responsibilities to his subordinates and bureaucrats. Thus each bureaucrat and minister will have his/her well documented, transparent target for each year. His/her performance could be assessed by the same agencies and monetary incentives could be provided for achievers and punishments for losers.

When the administration of the state becomes a managerial exercise, with its responsibilities, accountability and pains, its existing glamour quotient will naturally dissipate. The people of the Media can stop following them day and night, with cameras, in search of downright despicably scintillating news.

This single media act was chiefly instrumental in converting plain country administration into a glamour business of politics. It has also converted these purely managerial occupations of country governance into a fantastic, parallel world of glitz and glamour, which was totally unmatched with its democratic values and traditions.

If run like a plain managerial exercise, at the end of each term of a government, people will be easily able to judge the better performers, and decide wisely when their votes are asked for the next time.

The Media will also be able to concentrate more on meaningful social themes when they get free from the routine act of following leaders day and night. The Media's absence will itself distract many leaders from chasing political careers. Thus, the wasteful exercise of politics could be slowly eliminated from the scene of the country's administration.

Such a shift of priorities will get democracy reinvented into a rational, no non-sense managerial exercise the sacred purpose for which it was intended. The media should wake up, and take up the cause of reinventing democracy, and help it to become a national agenda.

Article: 9

A model of democracy without a political party system

<u>'Reinvented democracy': Can Democracy get rid of its political party system?</u>

As we all know well, a political party system was an accident that happened in the development of democracy during America's experiment with the great ideal. Thomas Jefferson and Hamilton had great differences of opinion about the economic direction of the government; whether to nurture big industries in the country or to be happy with the smaller ones or whether to be a highly industrialized nation or remain as an agrarian nation. This is where the USA's existing two party political system started, the Republicans and the Democrats.

This accident has resulted in transforming all future democracies into a plethora of political parties of all colours and shape. Democracy has turned a 100% political game among political parties, like in the olden day gang wars among tribal groups, for territorial supremacy. Here the most central theme of such wars has become the formation of the government, and remaining in power.

If the battle for the crown and the related bloody coups were prevalent among royal family groups in the past, today it is enacted by these political entities. Every other purpose of democracy has been dumped into the segment of mere 'means' in the enactment of the above primary game.

The energies involved are different, values are different and the laws of the game are also different. But still, out of ignorance of the masses, the new game is celebrated as the great democratic ideal, simply on the grounds that it is being played by the members of our own species of men, not by kings and feudal lords. Fortunately for us, its most popular definition does not demand anything more than - 'of the people, by the people, for the people'.

Can't our enlightened age engage us to revisit its foundational principles and reinvent it, so that it becomes a rational system capable of redefining man's life on the planet?

1. <u>**Let us look a possible new model of democracy :**</u>

   1) Introduce a specialized course for democracy from

plus-2 level (Pre-University) with the scope of continuing it up to PG (Post Graduation), or even doctoral level. Engage the best of educators to compile the course materials, with all the IMPLIED goals, meaning, dimensions and practice of democracy. This means that it should not merely consist of the history of democracy, but the theoretical and philosophical aspects of a true peoples' government. It should explore all its possibilities to redefine man's life, considering its potential to carry mankind much further in the path of civilization.

2) Introduce competitive exams among the qualified citizens to select the best 'members of parliament'(MPs) and 'members of the Legislative assembly'(MLAs) from each constituency.

3) Select the best from each existing constituency irrespective of national grades, to ensure proper representation – in other words, those who topped each constituency on the exams would become an MP/MLA from such a constituency. The existing quota system could be followed for such selections, if needed.

4) These members could elect their PM/CM (Prime Minister/ Chief Minister), and such a PM/CM (Prime Minister/ Chief Minister) can form his cabinet.

5) For each ministry, an expert committee consisting of the best qualified and experienced professionals in the country should be formed to help the Ministers in decision making.

6) Till this system comes into place, existing systems of political parties can continue with the same system, say for a maximum of two or three terms (total 15 years).

7) Financial decision making should be strictly de-linked from the authority of any single person or group. Our enlightened minds can find an imaginative solution for this problem.

8) Each constituency can have a citizen's council/ or a well reformed existing 'Panchayat'(village councils) system to work as a meaningful people's link with the MLAs / MPs.(Member of legislative assembly/member of parliament)   The election system can continue at this level so that people's representation is ensured at grass root level, doing true justice to the principles of direct democracy.

9) Each assembly can select its 'devils advocates' from among its members for the term of the assembly, to serve the purpose of a healthy opposition. This kind of an opposition without any political ambition would ensure healthy debates, with the sole purpose of arriving at the truth, and the best of courses. Now, from day one, the singular goal of the opposition is to dethrone the existing government, a very negative trait of the present day democracy. The goal of government formation must be taken away from groups to save democracy.

Our enlightened minds in the country could modify this basic idea gradually into a perfect system in due course. The media is doing an excellent job in exposing corruption and mistakes in governance. But it serve the purpose of only institutionalizing these symptoms today, as ever present, permanent features of the system. Hence, common sense calls for a look at the foundational blue-print the great ideal of democracy.

Only our media can start such an initiative for a reinvented democracy, by calling upon the public to open up their minds. A silent intellectual exercise predominantly involving open minded political leaders, intelligent men and members of the judiciary will then naturally follow.

How does the lack of adequate thrust in implementing Fraternity Clause in governance affects the life of citizens ?

Through time immemorial, man was under oppression and all kinds of subjugation under the reign of Kings, Feudal Lords and foreign invaders. He never had a chance to taste pure individual freedom and dignity. Democracy was an opportunity. But democracy also took over the old concept of 'the evil of political government' with its fear and authority oriented machinery, which was instrumental in the old subjugation of men.

Though fathers of our constitution had placed **Fraternity clause** (about INDIVIDUAL DIGNITY)as one of the DIRECTIONAL MOTIVES of the very existence of the state, along with liberty and equality, this one has received the least relevance and attention in country governance.

The police slap any citizen at will on the road, tax men con and extort citizens selectively; village officers and district collectors behave as if they were no different in power and authority from their predecessors under the old regimes. Political leaders sway their feeble minds here and there in the name of religion, or any other available ploy to extract mandate. His applications and complaints pile up in government offices every day, unopened, unseen and without any action having been taken. He is despised and scorned in government offices.

Government officers dare to trample upon the citizen this way chiefly because they know that he is the most irrelevant and helpless item in democracy. His cries will reach no where. It may take even up to two decades for justice to reach him if some one dares to complain to our law courts.

In what all ways the governmental indifference towards her citizens' prime existential need of INDIVIDUAL DIGNITY influence his character, personality, and their relation with the fellow citizens are described below :

a) The anxiety of every man that his self-hood and dignity is constantly under threat from the hands of the government agencies like the police, men from the tax offices, office of the department of electricity and water works, municipality etc., is very real. The police are the frontal face of every state. Their attitude towards a citizen is the general attitude of the state towards its citizen. **This fundamental fear that one's 'self' is in constant threat makes every one acquiring an 'aggressive' temper, or constitution. This is the hall mark of our age. Even nations are possessed by this constant mutual fear !**

b) When something is extremely difficult to safe-guard and maintain, man tends to abandon it for the sake of being free. Thus, the common man has abandoned his feeling of self worth in the country, as it is extremely difficult to up-keep, with out its being frequently violated in the course of his civic life !

 Its abandoning has become a practical necessity, and a kind of 'negative value' in the mainstream course of life. Even from schools and colleges, what every child tries hard to learn is this difficult negative value of abandoning one's self-respect. The easiest way to learn it is by not respecting his fellow beings, by calling him names, taunting and being violent towards him. With the assistance of such tricks, and by taking and giving insult, everyone tries to gain 'IMMUNITY' from verbal, and if possible from physical assault from his fellow beings.

 Such immunity is the most desired negative 'possession' or asset that every young man in the country ardently desires. No one can refute this day to day reality about modern life. **This is nothing but freedom from morality**! One who fails to acquire this quality of roughness and toughness is considered to be weak and vulnerable. He gets often targeted in ragging incidents etc. If anyone manages to grow up without these negative values, as a principled individual, he will find it extremely hard to perform at his job among his corrupt colleagues, whether in a private or a government job. Stories of the plights of such honest officers and political leaders are often heard in the media.

c) The madness to amass wealth and political power is a shield against such fear and threat. It is nothing but a neurosis for protecting one's personal freedom and dignity. There is no need for super intelligence to realize that money and power begets respect in our society. Respect means freedom from violation of one's dignity at the hands of the police, or any agents of government machinery. An example of Bihar is often quoted to prove this point. The maximum civil service aspirants have been from this state until recent years. Feudal system and caste related subjugation was at its most extreme in this state. Hence ordinary men are more neurotic to gain power and freedom that the civil service provides.

It is like a great flood. Politics and money are like rare dry mounts where one can escape the humiliation of being a common man in the country, and hence the national neurosis for money and power. We feel that this observation could be true for the entire world, as Democracy failed to upgrade man to his respectful status in society anywhere in the world. It has ended up as an open, plain game among political professionals for grabbing governmental power and the enjoyment of its traditional fruits.

Democracy has become mere a means in the hands of a few, to keep its traditionally acclaimed fruits of freedom for themselves ! To end this tragedy, world need to REINVENT DEMOCRACY so that it exist primarily to ensure and guarantee citizens' individual dignity in governance. This was the singular goal that mankind had intended to achieve from democracy. The mad craving for political power will end only when democracy enables itself to provide this primary need of man. Only a free man with adequate self-worth could value his fellow men, and pave way for peaceful community living in the world.

d)   **The lack of initiative, sense of duty and responsibility among government servants**: We talk endlessly on the lack of effectiveness and initiative of our government servants in the country's administration. But we always ignore that the central reason behind it is the lack of self respect and feeling of dignity of our government servants as individuals. When one has no respect for one's own self, his work will also be of a similar low quality. We have already seen the cause of this tragedy in the beginning. Government servants are no exception from the above disease in the country.

e)   **Lack of a sense of reason and scientific spirit**: Freedom of the mind is an essential ingredient for one to think rationally, as only freedom will make an 'individual' in the true sense of the word. A person without a basic individual dignity can never think rationally as he is merely a dead log, meek and resigned to his fate.

f)   **Lack of cleanliness and a hygienic culture**: When one feels un-clean and incomplete about himself, with a zero sense of individual dignity, he will treat his surroundings also in the same way. He never develops a true sense of personal and community cleanliness. Hence we have heaps and heaps of garbage accumulated in our streets and markets, despite the existence of municipalities and corporations. When one is dirt inside, he loses his ability to distinguish between what is dirt and clean outside.

g) **Growing trend of fundamentalism**: Our generally obedient nature indirectly leaves us as highly authoritarian as well. We always expect the same obedience from others too, and get furious in the absence of it. Free self-expression never gets encouraged in such societies, and as a result, leaving all of us as fundamentalists in nature. A fundamentalist hates to think on his own, but takes the easy way of waiting for orders from the top, or the dictates of a traditional society. Our bullying bosses in offices are nothing but fundamentalists, as they are intolerant. We are yet to learn the habit of treating the 'other person' with the same respect as we would want the other to treat us with, irrespective of his or her socio-economic status.

h) **Lack of values in society**: Let us compare human values to flowers and fruits that comes out naturally when the plant gets adequate sunlight, space and manure. It is a natural outcome when all these ingredients are made available to the plants. Likewise, values naturally would flow from individuals when he has his space in society, and when his self respect and individual dignity is kept in-tact by the state governing mechanism.

Every form of government in the world is said to be aiming at achieving this ultimate goal i.e. to convert its people into enlightened, free, self respecting individuals. The preamble of our constitution too has these ideals clearly specified as the very motto of the existence of the state. But sadly, ignoring this central necessity, governments in developing countries put all their efforts and attention in ensuring the economic development of its people, completely ignoring this aspect of individual growth, or their blossoming into complete, dignified, self-respecting, free, enlightened individuals! Thus, the poor and the under privileged are kept and fed in the country as if they were in some super refugee camp !

If the atmosphere in the family determines an individual's value system, the country too plays an important role in the moulding that of its citizens.

We have no doubt about the family's role in the character building of an individual. Then why should we have doubt about the country's role in the character building and value orientation of its citizens? The character of the citizen is fully dependent upon the way the government behaves, and treats the people. There is nothing wrong in attributing a parents' role to the state in this meaning. The state is nothing but the sacred abode of the collective wisdom, reason and common sense of its people in its correct democratic sense.

Hence, a thorough review as to how effectively we could implement our FRATERNITY clause in the constitution and in day to day governance should be undertaken by all concerned institutions, enlightened minds, media, universities and top leaders in the country.

Liberate the other in order to achieve sustainable freedom for all

Is it the old jungle law that still rules the world?

It seems yes !

The law of the jungle was very simple. It was the rule of the strongest. Whether in the matter of having food, a mate or a resting place, it was the privilege of the strongest to be the first. If anyone else wanted all those privileges, he was free to have it, by defeating the former.

The single criterion for having this kind of upper-hand on everything was PHYSICAL STRENGTH.

A change happened to this singular criterion of physical strength at later stages, at least in the history of the species of man. The less strong could group together, gathering the strength of many, to defeat the strongest single member in the group. This grouping together did not happen naturally. It required the leadership skills of someone from the group of the less strong. Instead of the superiority in physical strength, an element of the mind had emerged in the scene. A mind that was capable of uniting the oppressed to fight the strongest. He was more a strategist than a physically strong man. This quality was respected in the same way that physical strength was respected in the jungle. Instead of the strongest man in the group, now the strongest leader with the largest or the bravest followers is respected in human societies. These leaders have become invaders and war-lords in the history of the world.

This man of the mind was shrewd enough to keep all the other strong men in the tribe with him, in the fold. It was a natural fraternity of all the strong men. The original spirit behind the grouping of the oppressed class of men to defeat the strongest in the group has taken a retreat here. Hereon, the phenomenon of men's grouping in history would always be the grouping of strongmen for supremacy in societies. Even if the original form of grouping of the less strong with the original spirit had occurred at times, it was always later taken over by the strong men as their own, for achieving their goals.

When collective strength of the group couldn't save men from natural calamities, wide-spread diseases and famine, the religious man had taken over the leadership of human societies in between, claiming his supernatural connections. He became all powerful in matters of both war and peace. The hegemony behind being a Brahmin in Indian societies, and the long reign of the Church in Europe are best examples of this phenomenon. In Europe, the head of the Church has even the rights and privileges for appointing Kings.

The criterion for social leadership has again taken a marked deviation from the period of Industrial revolution in Europe. A new category of powerful men has started emerging in the scene, in the form of the manufacturer-trader class. Besides the leadership skill required for the old kind of social-upper-hand, this new class had the special gift of 'business acumen' as well, to claim their superiority in a society. It has become the most admired quality in modern societies henceforth.

The attraction of the adventurous travels to the new overseas markets and the exotic items brought from these mysterious foreign lands by these new classes were so powerful that, it is said, the British high society members were even willing to exchange their knighthood and similar honours to acquire them. Many European Kings and rulers, in collaboration with these new trading classes, could free themselves from the clutches of the all powerful Church during this period, and bring an end to the era of the supremacy of the Church in the world.

Luckily or unluckily for the world, this new class of businessmen never attempted to take over political thrones for themselves. They preferred to remain in the background, and finance the operations of the political class instead. How the East India Company, a private company initially, had come under the direct operations of the British Empire is part of recorded history. The phenomenon of the grouping of all the strongest for achieving the common goal is seen here again.
Freedom as a right of men was rarely demanded by ordinary people in history. The Magna Carta treaty, which was a treaty where human kind heard for the first time wonderful concepts like those about 'Freedom', was demanded from the Kings by the then Nobles. The King was arbitrarily confiscating ships and cargo of the Nobles who were in trade. The treaty was forcibly signed from the King under threat of military action, by the group of Nobles.

The House of Commons was also introduced in England with the active help of the House of Lords, who wanted to reduce the power of the King in collaboration with the new rich class of Traders. Thus the seeds of democracy were never sown by genuine class of 'people' during its re-emergence in the modern world, but undertaken by other parallel classes of powerful people, who wanted to take over political power from the hands of its former masters, and control it as their exclusive right. **It has always been a changing of political and social authority from the hands of one master to the other**.

This old facts about democracy is unfortunately alive and active even today. It remains in the hands of the active and powerful professional political leaders, and the business class. **Hence the reign of the powerful over the hapless common man still continues** . A passive media, willing to dance to the tunes of any current master, whoever they are, help the system to thrive in the world, without obstructions.

The natural urge behind anyone or any group, trying to have control over their surroundings, including control over the people around, is their universal urge for having Freedom. The more they have control over others, the more they will be free to have their way. Keeping the 'other' free is always considered a risk and threat that, some day, he may attempt to subjugate the former. This fear of the other 'abducting' own freedom unless his freedom is kept under check, lies as the bottom energy beneath all our existing political systems in the world, including democracy. Hence, every nation arms itself to its capacity to ward of others from attacking it ! Hence, the only way for peace in communities, and the world as a whole is to discard the above mutual fear !World as a whole has to realize the need to liberate the other first, so that his fear is mitigated about our attacking him first.

The universal urge for Freedom of one and all will be active all the time, irrespective of the age in which one lives, hence the suppressed will always rise-up against the oppressor, with the goal of mitigating him, if possible for ever. Man's history so far has manifested on numerous occasions the fact that no population can be permanently kept under suppression and control. Revolutions and bloody revolts will always erupt to annihilate such oppressors.

Hence, man's collective common sense must rise to realize that, sustainable freedom for the world is possible only by liberating the other person. The unchangeable law for having one's permanent freedom and the freedom of human societies in general is liberating the other by each individual, and liberating larger societies by state institutions.

Only a liberated man would be able to realize the worth of Freedom, and then liberate all others around him. Our civilization on earth would deserve to be called truly civilized only when our socio-economic and political institutions realize this simple natural law, and set right their ways. So, a reinvented DEMOCRACY is world's singular means to achieve this end. Mankind could reinvent men's lives only by first reinventing its political system of democracy, making it a tool to liberate all men in all respect. Such a reinvented democracy only could teach every citizen the lesson of liberating every other man, so that communities and nations could relish the joy of collective freedom, ending the prevailing trend of every one fearing the other.

-----------------------end----------------------------